STORY OF THE
TITANIC

ILLUSTRATION: STEVE NOON

CONSULTANT: DR ERIC KENTLEY

**London, New York,
Melbourne, Munich, and Delhi**

Senior Editor Francesca Baines
Senior Art Editor Sheila Collins
Editor Matilda Gollon
Managing Editor Linda Esposito
Managing Art Editor Diane Peyton Jones
Category Publisher Laura Buller
Picture Researcher Susie Peachey
Production Editor Tony Phipps
Senior Production Controller Angela Graef
Jacket Designer Laura Brim
Design Development Manager Sophia M Tampakopoulos Turner

DK India
Assistant Art Editor Neha Sharma
Senior Art Editor Sudakshina Basu
Managing Art Editor Arunesh Talapatra
Deputy Managing Editor Pakshalika Jayaprakash
DTP Manager Balwant Singh
DTP Designer Anita Yadav

First published in Great Britain in 2012 by
Dorling Kindersley Limited,
80 Strand, London WC2R 0RL
Copyright © 2012 Dorling Kindersley Limited
A Penguin Random House Company

10 9
020–183840 – 03/12

A CIP catalogue for this book is available
from the British Library.

ISBN: 978-1-40938-339-0

Hi-res workflow proofed by MDP, UK
Printed and bound by
Leo, China

Discover more at
www.dk.com

CONTENTS

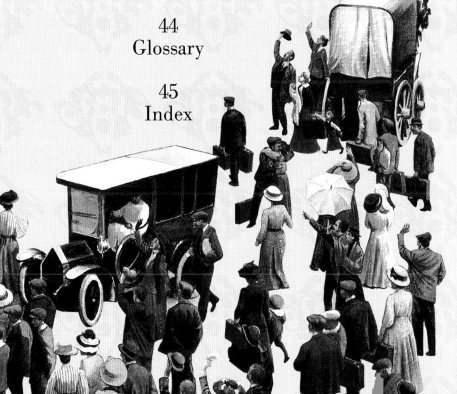

THE SHIP OF DREAMS

In the late nineteenth and early twentieth centuries, millions of people emigrated from Europe to North America. The only way to cross the Atlantic Ocean is by ship, and two of the biggest shipping companies are Cunard and the White Star Line. Cunard have the fastest ships, so the White Star Line have decided to build new ships that are the biggest and most luxurious in the world. The first is the *Olympic*; the second is her sister ship, the *Titanic*.

WELCOME TO AMERICA

For most passengers, the journey to America is a one-way trip to escape poverty or oppression in Europe and start a new life. In New York Harbour, immigrants are welcomed by the Statue of Liberty, a symbol of freedom and hope. Between 1900 and 1914, more than 12 million people immigrated in this way.

THE PASSENGERS ON BOARD

More than 2,200 people are sailing on the *Titanic's* maiden voyage (first trip). As well as 1,324 passengers, there are 898 crew. Here are just some of the people on board. Follow their different fates as the story of the *Titanic* unfolds.

Thomas Andrews is the managing director of Harland and Wolff, the company that built the *Titanic*. He is also the ship's chief designer and knows every little detail about it. He is coming along on the maiden voyage to check that everything is running well and to note any changes that need to be made. He is a popular man and incredibly hard-working. He has spent the previous week noting improvements that would make the *Titanic* even more luxurious.

Edward John Smith is the captain of the *Titanic*. As the White Star Line's most experienced officer, his salary is twice that of other White Star captains. He is called the "Millionaire's Captain", because he is a favourite among society people. He has regular passengers who would not dream of crossing the Atlantic with any other captain. He has been transferred from the *Olympic*, the *Titanic's* sister ship. This will be his last voyage. After 26 years with the company, he plans to retire.

Sir Cosmo Duff Gordon is a Scottish aristocrat. He is travelling in first class with his wife, Lucile, a famous dress designer for fashionable London and New York society. She has urgent business in New York and has taken the first available ship. Lady Duff Gordon's career began when her first marriage ended, leaving her penniless with a young daughter. To economize, she made most of their clothes. Friends commented on the beautiful designs, and her reputation spread.

Joseph Bruce Ismay is the managing director of the White Star Line, the *Titanic's* owner and a company his father established. Ten years ago, Ismay sold the White Star Line to an American company called International Mercantile Marine, owned by J.P. Morgan, but retained his role of managing director and chairman. White Star Line ships are also still registered in Britain, fly the British flag, and have British crews.

THE MIGHTY *TITANIC*

The *Titanic* is truly vast. It is able to carry up to 3,547 passengers and crew. It will be the heaviest ship afloat – its volume fully laden will be 67,063 metric tons (73, 923 tons) – and also the finest. From bow to stern, the *Titanic* will measure 269 m (883 ft) – 22 double-decker buses placed end to end would fit along the deck.

LUXURY LINERS

For first-class passengers, the accommodation on board transatlantic liners rivals that of the finest hotels on land. No expense is spared, and every detail has been thought of, from the design of the large public rooms, some in the style of grand country houses, decorated with rare woods, marble, and gold leaf, down to the quality of the soap in the bathrooms.

Agnes Sandström is 24. She has been visiting relatives in her native Sweden. She is now going back to the US, where she lives with her husband in San Francisco. She is travelling in third class with her two young daughters, Marguerite (4) and Beatrice (20 months). They board the *Titanic* at Southampton and share a cabin with another Swedish family. Of the 497 third-class passengers boarding, 180 are Scandinavian.

Michel Navratil, a tailor from France, has a secret. He is travelling under the false name of Louis Hoffman with his two sons, Michel (3) and Edmond (2). He is separated from his wife, but his sons stayed with him over the Easter weekend. When his wife came to pick the boys up, they had disappeared. Michel Navratil is running away with his sons to start a new life in the US. They board the *Titanic* at Southampton and are travelling second class.

Colonel John Jacob Astor is the richest first-class passenger of all. His fortune includes the Astoria Hotel in New York. He is also an inventor and invented a bicycle brake and a device for flattening road surfaces. Colonel Astor is returning to the US after a long holiday with his young wife, Madeleine, who is expecting a baby. They board the *Titanic* at Cherbourg, France, with his manservant, Mrs Astor's maid, a nurse, as well as their pet dog, Kitty.

Fifth Officer Harold Lowe is a 28-year-old officer from Wales. He has wanted to be a sailor since he was a child, and he ran away to sea when he was 14. He has no formal education, but he earned his certificates at sea. He joined the White Star Line just 15 months ago. Before that, he spent five years on steamers on the coast of West Africa. This will be his first trip across the Atlantic. Lowe is a conscientious and plain-spoken officer.

GRAND DESIGNS

The *Olympic* and the *Titanic* are the big idea of Lord William Pirrie, chairman of the Belfast shipyard Harland and Wolff, and Joseph Bruce Ismay, chairman of the White Star Line. Their dream is to build vast, luxurious liners that will outshine their rivals. The *Olympic* is the first of the new liners to be built, and a few months later, on 31 March 1909, construction of the *Titanic* begins.

HARLAND AND WOLFF
The White Star Line have always used the shipyard of Harland and Wolff in Belfast, Northern Ireland, to build their ships. Harland and Wolff are the biggest employer in the city, and for the construction of the *Olympic* and the *Titanic*, the workforce doubles.

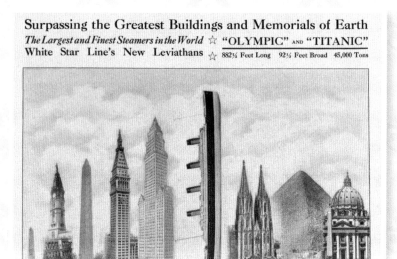

Surpassing the Greatest Buildings and Memorials of Earth
The Largest and Finest Steamers in the World ☆ "OLYMPIC" and "TITANIC"
White Star Line's New Leviathans ☆ 882½ Feet Long 92½ Feet Broad 45,000 Tons

1 Bunker Hill Monument, Boston — 221 Feet High
2 Public Buildings, Philadelphia — 534 Feet High
3 Washington Monument, Washington — 555 Feet High
4 Metropolitan Tower, New York — 700 Feet High
5 New Woolworth Building, New York — 750 Feet High
6 White Star Line's Triple Screw Steamers "OLYMPIC" and "TITANIC" — 882½ Feet Long
7 Cologne Cathedral, Cologne, Germany — 516 Feet High
8 Grand Pyramid, Gizeh, Africa — 451 Feet High
9 St. Peter's Church, Rome, Italy — 448 Feet High

BIGGER AND BETTER
The White Star Line are keen to advertise the vast scale of their new liners. One of their brochures compares the *Olympic* and *Titanic* steamships to some of the tallest buildings in the world, including the Great Pyramid of Giza, Egypt.

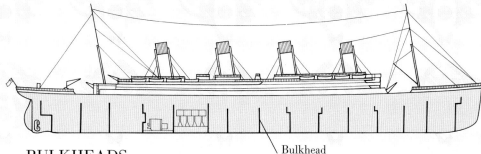

Bulkhead

BULKHEADS
To increase its safety and strengthen the hull, the *Titanic* has 15 bulkheads (vertical partitions) that divide the ship into 16 compartments. In the event of an accident in which two compartments are flooded, the theory is that the ship will still float. However, the bulkheads reach only 3 m (10 ft) above the waterline, and water would be able to spill over the top of one compartment to another.

ON THE SLIPWAY
The huge size of the new liners means that special slipways (ramps) have to be built. To launch the ships, the slipways are covered with vast quantities of soft soap, tallow (animal fat), and tallow mixed with oil.

UNSINKABLE?

Although it is said that the *Titanic*'s designers claim she is unsinkable, this is not true. Harland and Wolff said that the system of bulkheads "made the vessel virtually unsinkable", but the word "virtually" appears to have been forgotten. In fact, other ships have survived collisions with icebergs. In 1879, the *Arizona* (left) hit an iceberg head-on off Newfoundland, and made it back home.

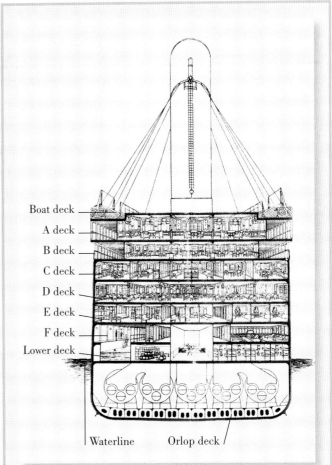

Boat deck
A deck
B deck
C deck
D deck
E deck
F deck
Lower deck

Waterline   Orlop deck

CROSS-SECTION

This cross-section of the hull gives a good idea of the box-like shape and construction of the *Titanic*. The distance from the boat deck to the waterline was 18.4 m (60.5 ft). Beneath the waterline was the orlop deck, and the engines and boilers that drove the ship.

A WARNING SIGN?

On 20 September 1911, the *Olympic* collided with the warship HMS *Hawke*. Both ships were badly damaged, and the *Olympic*, under the command of Captain Edward J Smith, was found to be at fault. A year later, Captain Smith was put in charge of the *Titanic*.

FRIDAY
10
MARCH
1911

BUILDING THE *TITANIC*

At the Harland and Wolff shipyard in Belfast, more than 11,300 people are busy at work on the *Titanic*. The yard rings with the sound of hammers, and shakes with the thunder of heavy equipment. Work began two years ago, and the empty hull is almost ready for the launch, planned for 31 May 1911, when the ship will be pulled by tugs into dry dock and fitted out.

Welders

Welder

Painters

Timber shoring

Rudder

Jetty wall

SPEED 5 KNOTS

Well for propeller

Steam truck

MIGHTY MACHINES

Newly invented hydraulic machines are used to rivet many of the steel plates together.

STEEL PLATES

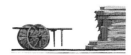

More than 2,000 steel plates, most 9 m (30 ft) long, are fixed together by three million rivets.

DOUBLE PROTECTIO

The Titanic has a double-bottomed hull, with a gap of up to 2.1 m (7 ft) between the layers.

PROGRESS UPDATE
Can you find chief designer Thomas Andrews discussing progress with Joseph Bruce Ismay, the White Star chairman?

TAKING A BREAK
Two workers have managed to slip away and take a crafty break from their work. Can you spot them?

A FRIENDLY FACE
The shipyard is busy day and night, and a stray cat tries its luck, begging scraps from the workmen.

Revolving crane

Lift

Access ramp

Shored-up decks

E deck
F deck
G deck
Space for engine

Double bottom

Portholes

Plater's shed for cutting steel plates for hull

River Lagan

SLIPWAY SCAFFOLD
The giant gantry – the scaffold structure around the ship – is 256 m (840 ft) long and 73 m (240 ft) wide.

HORSEPOWER
Horse and cart is the main means of transport. It takes 20 horses to carry the ship's huge main anchor.

SOARING CRANES
The gantry supports many cranes, including a revolving crane that towers above the skyline.

A FLOATING PALACE

Workmen swarm all over the *Titanic* as she is transformed into a fully equipped floating palace. The attention to detail is breathtaking. There are stained-glass windows, carved wooden panelling, chandeliers, rich carpets, and fine furniture. Electric lighting and heating are also being installed, along with modern electric lifts. It will take 10 months to fit the ship out.

Electric crane

Carpenters

Welder

Bridge

Carpets

Pullman bunk

1st-class room

D deck

Scotland Road

Sink

3rd-class room for 6

E deck

Painting squash court

Building bunks

F deck

Boiler uptake taking waste gas to funnel

3rd-class room

Building bunks

G deck

Boiler room no. 6

POWERHOUSE

Twenty-nine boilers arranged in six boiler rooms are needed to provide the steam power for the engine.

LIFEBOAT CAPACITY

In all, there are 14 lifeboats, two emergency lifeboats, and four collapsible lifeboats – enough for 1,178 people.

FINE FITTINGS

Most of the top four decks are for first-class passengers. Each first-class room is furnished in a different style of grandeur.

OUCH!
An army of men transport the furnishings – can you spot a man who has dropped a bed on his toe?

FINE FACILITIES
Every cabin has running water; however, there are only two bathtubs for all the 700 third-class passengers.

WORK INSPECTION
Thomas Andrews is as busy as ever, here inspecting the sumptuous fittings in a first-class bedroom.

Whistle

Installing funnel

Davits (cranes for the lifeboats)

Installing davits and lifeboats

Floating crane

Fitting windows

Access gangway

Delivery wagons

Furniture for 1st-class rooms

Boiler room no. 5

Coal bunkers

Boiler room no. 4

SCOTLAND ROAD
A crew's passageway runs the length of the ship. It is named after a working-class street in Liverpool.

FIRST-CLASS FUN
Painters decorate the squash court. There is also a gymnasium, a swimming pool, and a Turkish bath.

A SECRET PUFF
One of the workmen is hiding in a linen cupboard, where he is smoking a cigarette. Can you find him?

TUESDAY
9
APRIL
1912

LOADING WITH SUPPLIES

The *Titanic* is in Southampton, where she has been since 3 April. Here she is loaded with cargo and all the food she will need for all the people on board. The majority of the crew are recruited from Southampton, and families are saying their goodbyes to those of her 899 crew members still to board. Tomorrow, the *Titanic* leaves for New York on her maiden voyage – her first trip.

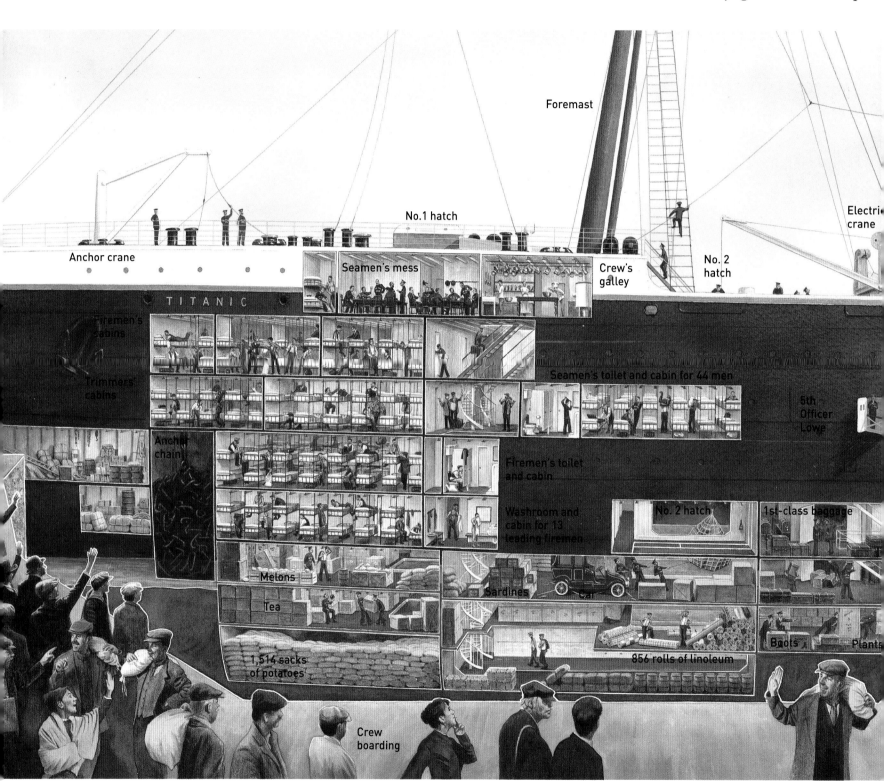

Foremast

No.1 hatch

Electric crane

Anchor crane

Seamen's mess

Crew's galley

No. 2 hatch

TITANIC

Firemen's cabins

Trimmers' cabins

Seamen's toilet and cabin for 44 men

5th Officer Lowe

Anchor chain

Firemen's toilet and cabin

Washroom and cabin for 13 leading firemen

No. 2 hatch

1st-class baggage

Melons

Sardines

Car

Tea

Boots

Plants

1,514 sacks of potatoes

856 rolls of linoleum

Crew boarding

FOREBODING

One recruit has a strange feeling of foreboding and decides to turn round and go home. In all, 24 crew do not sail.

CHOOSING BUNKS

Trimmers (who break up coal) have separate cabins to firemen (who feed coal into the boilers).

MORE SALT?

The chefs perfect their recipes. The larders bulge with more than 50,000 kg (110,000 lbs) of meat and fish and 40,000 eggs.

A HELPING HAND
A new stewardess asks for directions. Only 19 of 494 stewards are female, and there are 23 women crew in total.

FOR THE RECORD
A photographer records the scene, watched by his dog. Can you spot three dogs on the quay?

WELCOME ABOARD
Conscientious Fifth Officer Lowe checks all the new members of the crew as they board.

Thomas Andrews inspecting lifeboats

Collapsible B

Captain Smith on the bridge

Port light

No. 2 emergency lifeboat

Boat deck

No. 4 lifeboat

No. 6 lifeboat

No. 8 lifeboat

3rd Officer

5th Officer Lowe

6th Officer

A deck

B deck

C deck

D deck

E deck

Bosun

Ship's carpenter (6)

Quartermasters

Stewards' toilet

Dishwashers (20)

2nd-class stewards (42)

Quayside (cutaway)

Photographer

Beer wagon

ALES

ON THE BRIDGE
Captain Smith surveys the busy scene from the bridge. He plans to retire after this final voyage.

ARGY-BARGY
With so many crew living close together, tempers sometimes fray. Can you spot two firemen arguing over a bunk?

IN THE HOLD
The ship is also transporting cargo, including 13 crates of feathers, four crates of hairnets, and one new car.

THE PASSENGERS BOARD

Passengers have been boarding the *Titanic* all morning. A boat train from Waterloo Station in London arrived at 9.30 am carrying second- and third-class passengers. Another train, carrying first-class passengers, is due at 11.30 am. Then, at midday, the *Titanic* will set sail.

Parlour suite

A steward serves Joseph Bruce Ismay's tea.

1st-class bedroom

1st-class bedroom

Living room

Bedroom

Lavatory

Bathroom

Bedroom

Captain Smith

1st-class reception

1st-class dining saloon

Stewards preparing for lunch

Engineer

WELCOME ABOARD
Captain Smith is a favourite of the rich and famous and personally greets all the first-class passengers.

FRESH PRODUCE
The ship is well stocked with food, including 7,000 lettuces and 2,500 kg (5,525 lb) of tomatoes.

LOYAL SERVANTS
Many first-class passengers bring their servants – maids, valets, and nannies for the children.

YOUNG PASSENGERS

There are 109 children aboard the *Titanic*. Can you spot this excited girl wearing a red dress?

UNDERCOVER

Can you see second-class passenger Louis Hoffman and his two sons? This Frenchman's real name is Navratil.

GOING HOME

Agnes Sandström and her two daughters are returning third class to America after a holiday in Sweden.

Docking bridge

1st-class Smoking Room

Palm Court

Poop deck

Thomas Andrews

1st-class promenade

Stewards carrying luggage

1st-class rooms

2nd-class entrance

1st-class bedrooms

2nd-class room

Baker

3rd-class room

Kitchen

Engineer's mess

Scotland Road

3rd-class entrance

Cook

LUXURY SUITE

The two promenade suites are the most expensive on board. Joseph Bruce Ismay, chairman of the White Star Line, has one.

DINING IN STYLE

The *Titanic's* largest room is its first-class dining saloon. Styled on a 17th-century stately home, it seats 550.

A QUICK NIP

The ship's bakers rise early to bake fresh bread each day. Can you spot someone having a crafty drink?

THE LAST PORT OF CALL

After a stop in Cherbourg, France, to pick up passengers, the *Titanic* arrives in Queenstown (now Cobh) in Ireland. She is too big to dock at the port and has to anchor more than 3 km (2 miles) offshore. A few passengers disembark, but another 120 join the ship, and 1,385 sacks of mail are loaded. Just after 1.30 pm, following a stay of only two hours, the *Titanic* sets sail for New York.

WHITE STAR LINE
The red flag of the White Star Line shows the distinctive company logo.

GOING ASHORE
The White Star Line's paddle steamers take passengers disembarking from the *Titanic* to shore.

BLUE ENSIGN
The blue ensign (flag) is flying because Captain Smith belongs to the British Royal Naval Reserve.

FREE RIDE
One of the crew deserts the ship. He lives in Queenstown and used the *Titanic* as a free trip home.

CAPTAIN SMITH
Can you spot Captain Smith? He is watching the scene from a solitary position at the back of the ship.

FAKE FUNNEL
Four funnels look impressive, but the rear one is a dummy, used as a ventilator, not a chimney.

FARE
First-class passengers have paid £4 ($6) for the crossing from Southampton to Ireland.

AMERICAN FLAG
The American flag is flying because the White Star Line was bought by an American company in 1902.

SELLING SOUVENIRS
Small boats with Irish linen, lace, and other souvenirs sail out to the ship to sell them to the passengers.

RELAXING AT SEA

A few days into the voyage, the passengers are relaxing. The different classes walk on different promenades, talk in separate lounges, and each eat in their own dining rooms. The swimming pool, gymnasium, and Turkish baths are for the exclusive use of first-class passengers. The most expensive suites are the promenade suites on B deck, one of which cost £512 ($2,493).

Serving tea

Reading and Writing Room

Hobby horse

1st-class lounge

1st-class promenade

1st-class dining saloon

1st-class dining saloon

3rd-class dining room

KEEP FIT
Between 1 pm and 3 pm, the gym, with its up-to-date equipment, is reserved only for children.

GOING DOWN
There are four lifts for the use of passengers: three in first class and one in second class.

TURKISH DELIGHT
The Turkish bath has hot, temperate, and cool rooms, and even separate rooms for shampooing.

PASS THE SALT
Sir Cosmo and Lady Duff Gordon enjoy a four-course luncheon in the first-class dining saloon.

HIDE-AND-SEEK
Life on board the busy ship is fun for children. Can you spot two kids playing hide-and-seek?

WARNING MESSAGE
Joseph Bruce Ismay has received a wireless message warning of ice ahead.

5th Officer Lowe

Glass dome

Rowing machines

Gymnasium

1st-class entrance and Grand Staircase

No. 5 lifeboat

No. 3 lifeboat

Joseph Bruce Ismay

A deck

Enclosed 1st-class promenade

B deck

Private promenade

Grand staircase

Electric lift

C deck

1st-class reception room

D deck

G deck

Mosaic floor

Turkish bath's cool room

Heated saltwater pool

PEACE AND QUIET
The reading room is popular with women. They write letters here or read a book from the library.

HAT OVERBOARD!
The wind has snatched a lady's hat and tossed it overboard. Can you see her – and her hat?

A GOOD DINNER
In third class, where the Sandströms eat lunch, there is not much choice, but portions are generous.

DINING ON BOARD

This evening, first-class passengers can enjoy an 11-course feast in the dining saloon, second-class passengers have a three-course meal, while beef stew, bread, and tea are served in third class. After eating, the more hardy take an evening stroll, but the temperature has dropped 10 degrees. Captain Smith is worried about ice and calls in at the bridge before going to bed at 9.20 pm.

Main mast

Electric cranes

Electric cranes

2nd-class promenade

3rd-class promenade

2nd-class promenade

Steward walking dogs on poop deck

2nd-class promenade

3rd-class general room

2nd-class cabin

2nd-class dining saloon

3rd-class

STARRY NIGHT

The ocean is calm, like a glass lake, and the temperature is just above freezing. People taking the air dress warmly.

PLAYROOM

In the evening, the Verandah Café becomes a playroom for young first-class passengers.

SINGING HYMNS

Mr Navratil and his sons attend hymn singing. Many hymns are about dangers at sea.

SEA DOGS

There are so many dogs on board the ship that a dog show is planned for 15 April.

TAKING LEAVE

Captain Smith leaves a party in his honour in the A la Carte Restaurant. He usually eats alone.

BACK TO WORK

After dinner, Thomas Andrews returns to his cabin to work, planning improvements to the ship.

No. 4 funnel

Glass dome

No. 15 lifeboat

No. 13 lifeboat

No. 11 lifeboat

The Astors

1st-class promenade

1st-class Smoking Room

1st-class entrance

Verandah Café and Palm Court

Restaurant reception

A la Carte Restaurant

Vicar leads hymns

Café Parisien

Café Parisien

1st-class rooms

Seating for 394 people

1st-class cabin

EEEK!

Passengers in the third-class general room are shocked to see a rat dash across the carpet.

CAFÉ PARISIEN

Café Parisien is a copy of a sidewalk café in Paris and has genuine French waiters.

MEN ONLY

First-class gentlemen passengers can retire to the Smoking Room for an after-dinner drink.

ICEBERG AHEAD!

In the crow's nest, two lookouts are scanning the sea for ice. Suddenly, a massive iceberg looms out of the darkness. They ring the alarm and telephone the bridge. First Officer Murdoch gives the order to reverse the engines and steer to port (left). He saves the ship from a head-on collision, but the iceberg scrapes the side of the ship, cutting into the hull below the waterline.

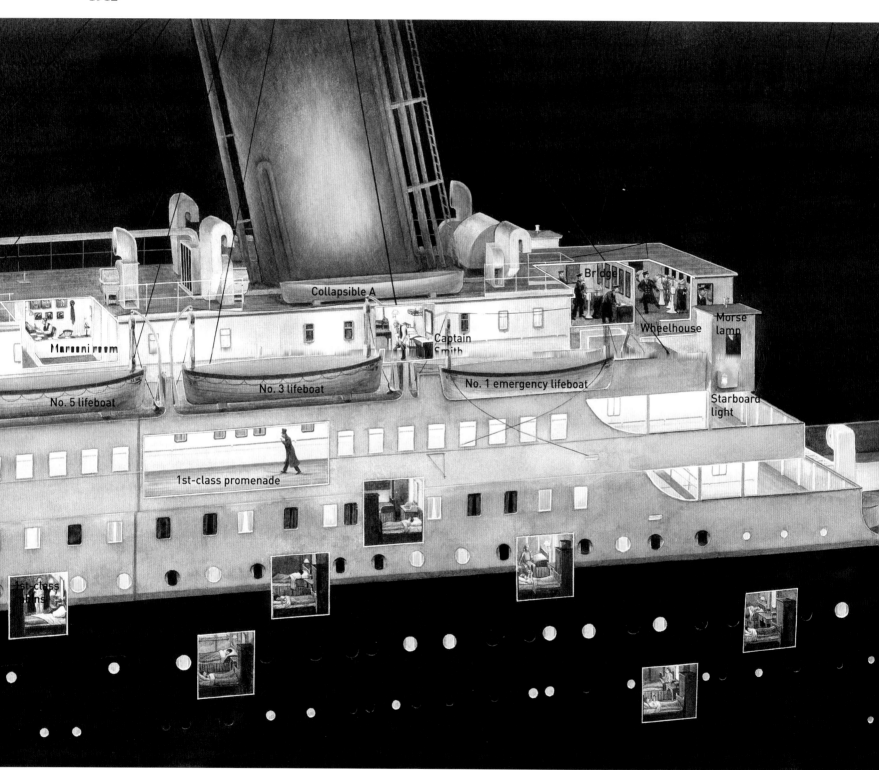

Collapsible A

Bridge

Captain Smith

Wheelhouse

Morse lamp

Marconi room

No. 5 lifeboat

No. 3 lifeboat

No. 1 emergency lifeboat

Starboard light

1st-class promenade

1st-class cabins

BUMP IN THE NIGHT
Captain Smith is woken by the sound of the iceberg scraping along the hull, and rushes to the bridge.

TAKING NOTE
Sixth Officer Moody notes down the time of the collision in the ship's log.

WIRELESS OFFICER
Wireless operator Jack Phillips is still at work, sending greeting messages from passengers.

AT THE WHEEL
Quartermaster Hichens has swung the wheel as far as he can, obeying First Officer Murdoch's orders.

LOOKING OUT
If they had been given binoculars, the lookouts might perhaps have seen the iceberg sooner.

BULKHEADS
Fearing the worst, Murdoch flips the switch to close the watertight doors of the bulkheads.

Forecastle deck

Firemen's mess

Firemen

Trimmers

3rd class

Greasers

3rd-class cabins

NIGHT VISION
The forecastle deck is kept in darkness to give the lookouts better visibility.

DEEP SLEEP
Many passengers sleep right through the collision with the iceberg.

PILLOW FIGHT
Can you find these two third-class passengers enjoying a pillow fight?

THE *TITANIC* IS DOOMED

Captain Smith calls Thomas Andrews to the bridge, and the two men make a quick tour of the ship. The iceberg has cut gashes in the hull over a length of 90 m (295 ft) long, and the first five bulkhead compartments are filling with water fast, pulling down the bow. It is clear to Andrews that the ship will sink in a few hours. Captain Smith gives the order to uncover the lifeboats.

14 APRIL 1912

No. 1 funnel

5th Officer Lowe

Gymnasium

1st-class promenade

Grand Staircase

Bridge and wheelhouse

1st class

1st class

1st class

Reception room

Purser's office

1st class cabin

1st class

Steward

1st class

Coal

Coal

Bulkhead

Boiler room no. 5

3rd class

Arguing over way out

Boiler room no. 6

Bulkhead

3rd class

Bulkhead

Post off

Mail sack

CONFUSION

Some third-class passengers can't find their way to the boat deck from their rooms low down in the hull.

FLOODED

The mailroom is flooding. The postal clerks are trying to move the mail sacks to the deck above.

QUEUING UP

Passengers form an orderly queue outside the purser's office to collect their valuables.

DECISION TIME

Captain Smith and Thomas Andrews take just 10 minutes to assess that the damage is enough to sink the ship.

WAITING ROOM

The Duff Gordons wait in the gym to escape the cold. People still believe the ship is unsinkable.

BAD NEWS

Stewards have been ordered to wake up the passengers. Everyone will be issued with a life jacket.

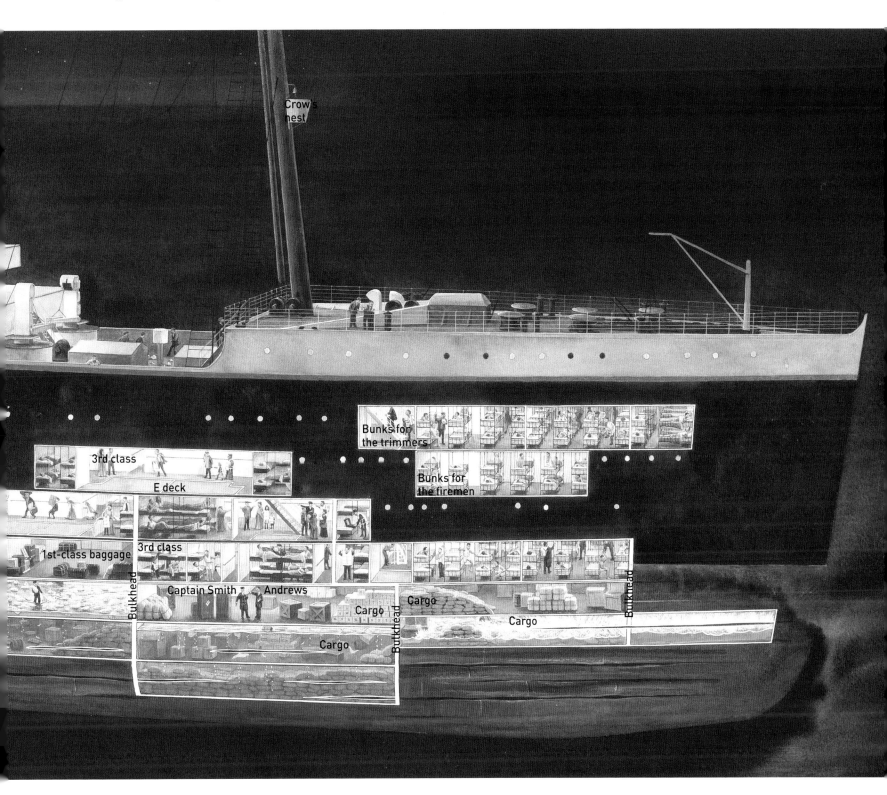

Crow's nest

Bunks for the trimmers

Bunks for the firemen

3rd class

E deck

1st-class baggage

3rd class

Captain Smith   Andrews

Cargo

Cargo

Cargo

Cargo

Bulkhead

Bulkhead

Bulkhead

LOOK AT THIS!

Can you spot the fireman waking up his mates to show them a lump of ice?

JUST IN CASE

Fifth Officer Lowe and other crewmen start taking the covers off the lifeboats, in case they are needed.

ICE FOOTBALL

Some passengers amuse themselves playing football with ice on the well deck.

THE LAST LIFEBOATS

The *Titanic* is sinking fast, and it is now clear that there are not enough lifeboats for all those left on board. The order is "women and children first", but many of the lifeboats have already been launched just half full. The wireless operators have been sending out distress signals to ships in the area – the only hope now is that a ship can reach the *Titanic* before she sinks.

15 APRIL 1912

No. 3 funnel

No. 2 funnel

2 boats remain on port side

Thomas Andrews

Gymnasium

Heading for stern

Lounge

Baker

Band playing on port side

Parting from father

1st-class dining saloon

Reception room

Grand Staircase

2nd class cabin

E deck

No. 3 lifeboat

LIFEBOAT NO. 1
The Duff Gordons and 10 others are in no. 1 lifeboat, even though it has capacity for 40 people.

COLLAPSIBLE C
As collapsible C lifeboat starts to be lowered, Joseph Bruce Ismay steps in.

SAVE MY SONS!
Mr Navratil searches desperately for space in a lifeboat so that his sons can be saved.

SOS

The wireless operators send out distress signals to other ships. It is one of the first times a ship uses the signal "SOS".

DON'T PANIC!

An officer fires his gun to stop passengers storming a lifeboat, as panic sets in.

GIVING ORDERS

Captain Smith orders the lifeboats to stand by, ready to return to pick up people from the water.

No. 1 funnel

Collapsible A

Bruce Ismay

Collapsible C

Marconi room

Saying goodbye

Men taken off boat

Bridge

Captain Smith

An officer fires distress rockets.

The Astors search for a lifeboat.

B deck

1st class cabin

C deck

D deck

Bow below water

No. 1 lifeboat

TO THE LIFEBOATS

Thomas Andrews searches the ship, urging passengers to put on life jackets, go on deck, and get into the lifeboats.

DECKCHAIRS

The chief baker throws deckchairs overboard, in the hope that people can use them as life rafts.

RAISING SPIRITS

The brave band play waltz and ragtime tunes to keep up everyone's spirits.

FINAL MOMENTS

All the lifeboats have gone. No ship has been able to reach the *Titanic* in time. The crowd of people on the stern have no hope of rescue now. As the bow sinks further and further, the stern is lifted higher and higher out of the water. Suddenly, a huge roar is heard as the ship breaks in two. In a few moments, the *Titanic's* lights will go out. The stern will rise until it is completely upright and then slide into the icy water.

COLLAPSIBLE B

Four collapsible lifeboats are stored, flat and upturned, on board. However collapsible B is washed off the deck before it can be launched, and lands in the water upside down. Thirty people manage to balance on it.

Collapsible C

Collapsible B

No. 4 lifeboat

Collapsible D

DOWN THE ROPES

A number of people try to jump ship by sliding down the lifeboat ropes, or leaping from the lower decks. Others jump into the water, hoping that they will be able to scramble aboard a lifeboat.

ICY WATER

Some people try to make rafts out of deckchairs. In the freezing water, most won't survive half an hour. However the ship's baker, fortified by whisky, steps into the water as the stern sinks, barely getting his hair wet, and survives for some time before finding room in a lifeboat.

CLINGING TO THE STERN

Many of the people still on board are clinging to the stern. But the stern is rising vertically, and no one will be able to hold on for much longer. One passenger in no. 8 lifeboat checks his watch. At 2.20 am, just two hours and 40 minutes after striking the iceberg, the *Titanic* finally sinks.

No. 13 lifeboat

No. 14 lifeboat

33

RESCUE AT LAST

On her way from New York to Gibraltar, the *Carpathia* receives the distress call from the *Titanic* just after midnight. Immediately, the *Carpathia*'s captain changes course and speeds as fast as he can towards the stricken ship, dodging icebergs all the way. But the *Carpathia* is 107 km (58 nautical miles) away and cannot reach the site until 3.35 am. At 4.10 am, number 2 emergency lifeboat is alongside and being unloaded. One by one, the others follow, but it is not until after 8 am that the last survivors board. In all, 706 people are rescued by the *Carpathia*.

15 APRIL
1912

NUMBER 4 LIFEBOAT
A seaman helps row no. 4 lifeboat. His pay, like that of all the *Titanic* crew, stopped at midnight. Also aboard is Mrs Astor, now a widow.

No. 9 lifeboat

No. 4 lifeboat

NUMBER 14 LIFEBOAT
Fifth Officer Lowe sails no. 14 lifeboat to the *Carpathia* with collapsible D in tow. He was the only one to go back and look for survivors, pulling four people from the sea. He also went to the rescue of collapsible A as it sank.

CLIMBING ABOARD
Able survivors, such as Ismay, climb aboard the *Carpathia*. The less able are winched on board. Some young children are scooped up in mail sacks.

WATCHING IN SILENCE
The *Carpathia*'s passengers watch the rescue while the crew stand ready to receive the survivors with blankets, food, and medical help.

No. 13 lifeboat

No. 1 lifeboat

CARPATHIA

Collapsible C

No. 14 lifeboat

Collapsible D

ABOARD THE *CARPATHIA*

Many ships in the North Atlantic had heard the *Titanic*'s distress call, and as the morning of 15 April progressed, several ships arrived at the scene to see if they could help, including one called the *Californian*. But it was too late. No other survivors were found. At 8.50 am, the *Carpathia* set off for New York.

CAPTAIN ROSTRON
In charge of the *Carpathia* was Captain Arthur Rostron. He was very experienced, having been at sea since the age of 13, and greatly respected by his crew. He won praise for his conduct in the rescue of the survivors.

ALL HANDS ON DECK
Both the crew and passengers on the *Carpathia* took care of the survivors, offering blankets and hot food and drinks. Some passengers were taken into cabins, while others huddled on deck. Despite all the activity, the ship was silent, as the horror of the disaster sank in.

MEDALS OF THANKS
Later, the survivors joined together to buy a silver cup for Captain Rostron and medals for his crew. Each medal (left) showed the *Carpathia* sailing through the ice, and on the back bore the crew member's name and the inscription: "Presented to the captain, officers, and crew of RMS *Carpathia*, in recognition of gallant and heroic services, from the survivors of the SS *Titanic*, April 15th 1912".

DESTINATION NEW YORK
It would take the *Carpathia* three days to reach New York. Her wireless operator worked around the clock to let anxious relatives know who had been saved. Joseph Bruce Ismay dictated a telegram to notify the White Star Line that the *Titanic* had gone down with a serious loss of life, but the *Carpathia*'s operator did not send this until 17 April.

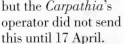

FIRST NEWS

The *Titanic*'s distress calls had alerted the world to the fact she was in trouble, but the story was not clear. The first newspaper reports stated that the *Titanic* was being towed to Halifax in Canada, but by 16 April, it was clear that this was a major disaster. Slowly, as telegrams from the *Carpathia* gave the names of the survivors, the horrific scale of the tragedy became clear.

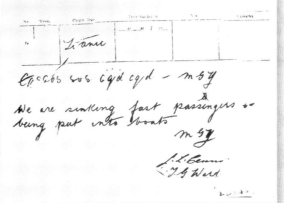

CONFUSION
The final radio message sent by the *Titanic* read, "We are sinking fast passengers being put into boats". There was nothing to suggest the true nature of the disaster. Captain Rostron waited until all survivors were safely on board the *Carpathia*, but it was not until that evening that he sent a telegram to the New York press confirming the worst.

"READ ALL ABOUT IT"
There was very little news from the White Star Line and the *Carpathia*, so friends and relatives searched the papers for any scrap of information that might tell them more about the fate of their loved ones.

ANXIOUS CROWDS
As news of the disaster filtered through, crowds of concerned relatives gathered outside the offices of the White Star in New York, London (above), and Southampton. It was some days before even an incomplete list of survivors was posted.

HEADLINES
The *Titanic* disaster dominated the world's newspapers for days, although many stories were vague and contradictory. Monday's New York *Evening Sun* even reported that all passengers were safe. People found it impossible to believe that such a tragedy could have occurred.

RETURN OF THE SURVIVORS

It was wet and gloomy when the *Carpathia* sailed into New York at 8 pm on 18 April. Confused by differing newspaper reports, a crowd of 40,000 people, among them frantic friends and relatives, waited on the dock for the survivors to disembark. Reporters jostled the dazed survivors, desperate for their stories. Some families were reunited with their loved ones, but for many more, their worst fears were confirmed.

ANXIOUS WAITING
Spotlights illuminated the crowd so that survivors might better see friends and relatives. As hope faded of finding their loved ones among the survivors, many in the waiting throng became hysterical with grief.

LIMPING HOME
Doctors and nurses stood by on the dock, ready to treat the injured and take them to hospital. Harold Bride, the wireless operator, had feet that were so frostbitten that he had to be carried ashore.

GRATEFUL SURVIVORS
Mrs Margaret Brown, a US millionairess who had taken charge of lifeboat no. 6 and helped with the injured on board the *Carpathia*, set up a survivors' committee and raised a large sum for those left destitute. She later presented a cup to Captain Rostron, on behalf of the grateful survivors.

REST IN PEACE
Many of the third-class passengers and crew who had not survived were buried at sea. On 20 April, at the scene of the disaster, Canon Kenneth Hind conducted a funeral service on board the ship the *Mackay-Bennett*. Further services were held over the following month as more victims were found.

THE ENQUIRIES

Two enquiries were held into the loss of the *Titanic*, one in the United States and one in England. The US enquiry lasted 18 days and the British hearing lasted 36 days. The 163 witnesses included White Star chairman, Joseph Bruce Ismay, Guglielmo Marconi, inventor of the radio telegraph system, lookout Frederick Fleet, and Captain Stanley Lord of the *Californian*.

THE US ENQUIRY
The US enquiry, seen here questioning Joseph Bruce Ismay, was very critical of Captain Smith, and questioned why the ship was going so fast through an ice field at night. This question remained unanswered. However, there was evidence that the *Titanic*'s crew had not been properly drilled in how to launch the lifeboats.

THE BRITISH ENQUIRY
The nearest ship to the *Titanic* that night was the *Californian*, and her crew were questioned at both enquiries as to why they did not come to the rescue. It was discovered that the *Californian*'s wireless operator did not hear the *Titanic*'s call for help because he was off duty.

RADIO CONTACT

Guglielmo Marconi (right) was one of the witnesses called to the stand at the US enquiry. The crucial role of the radio operators in the rescue of the survivors was noted. It was recommended that every ship must be equipped with a radio, and maintain radio contact 24 hours a day.

RECOMMENDATIONS
Important changes came out of the enquiries. The main recommendation was to make it compulsory for every ship to carry enough lifeboats for all the passengers and crew, and to hold regular lifeboat drills. Also as a result of the enquiries, an International Ice Patrol was set up in 1914, to look out for icebergs in North Atlantic shipping lanes. It still exists today.

LOST AND FOUND

The sinking of the *Titanic* took many lives and devastated a great many others. Many of the women and children who survived left husbands and fathers behind on the ship, and never saw them again. Agnes Sandström and her daughters survived, and were reunited with her husband in America, returning to live in Sweden, where he died some years later. However, she was one of the lucky ones.

THOMAS ANDREWS
Knowing how quickly the *Titanic* would sink, Thomas Andrews searched the ship that night, encouraging people to put on life jackets and get into the lifeboats. His last moments are a mystery. A steward saw him standing alone in the first-class Smoking Room, making no attempt to save himself. Others said they saw him on the boat deck, throwing deckchairs to people in the water, so they could use them as floats.

CAPTAIN SMITH
There are many stories about the fate of Captain Smith. Some survivors said they had seen him in the water. Others said he shot himself. Many people believe that he stayed on the bridge and went down with his ship.

HAROLD LOWE
Survivor Fifth Officer Lowe later reached the rank of commander in the Royal Naval Reserve. He never became a captain in the merchant service, and nor did any other officer who survived the sinking of the *Titanic*.

JOSEPH BRUCE ISMAY
As the *Titanic* sank, Joseph Bruce Ismay helped passengers into lifeboats. But as half-empty collapsible C was being lowered, he stepped in. Leaving the ship while women and children were still on board was seen as a cowardly act, and his reputation was ruined.

MANY HEROES
There were examples of great heroism that night. The musicians (right) played music, to keep the passengers' spirits up, and then went down with the ship. In the boiler rooms, the 24 engineers, worked to keep the lights burning to the last moment. None of them survived.

BRAVE AS THE "BIRKENHEAD" BAND: THE "TITANIC'S" MUSICIAN HEROES.

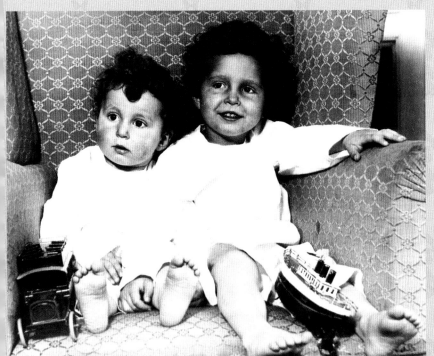

THE NAVRATIL BOYS
Michel Navratil managed to get his two boys into the last lifeboat that left the Titanic, but he did not survive himself. Pictures of the two French boys, dubbed "the orphans of the Titanic", were published all over the world. In Nice, France, Marcelle Navratil recognized them as her kidnapped sons and sailed immediately to be reunited with them.

THE ASTORS
Colonel Astor asked if he could accompany his pregnant wife in the lifeboat because of her "delicate condition". When refused, he stepped politely back. His body was recovered from the sea. Their baby son was born that August and named after his father.

THE DUFF GORDONS
Sir Cosmo and Lady Duff Gordon were saved in lifeboat no. 1, which carried a total of just 12 people. It was rumoured that Sir Cosmo had bribed crew not to return to save the drowning, for fear that their boat would be swamped. He was cleared of the accusations, but the very fact he had taken a space in the boat, in the place of women or children, ruined his name.

THE PEOPLE WHO DIED
There was no passenger list for the *Titanic*, and historians argue as to the precise number of people who died. The statistics in this book are based on the findings of the American enquiry. This graph shows how deaths varied greatly between the three classes and the crew.

	LOST	SAVED
1ST CLASS	130	199
2ND CLASS	166	119
3RD CLASS	536	174
CREW	685	214

SEARCH FOR THE *TITANIC*

Plans to find and recover the *Titanic* began immediately after the sinking, but the water in the North Atlantic was too deep. It was not until the late 1970s that the technology existed to go down to such depths. In 1985, a joint US/French expedition, led by Dr Robert Ballard, began a detailed search of the area using an unmanned submersible with video cameras. On 1 September, after weeks of exploring the murky seabed, the video monitor showed an image of one of the *Titanic*'s boilers. The ship had been found.

GHOST SHIP
The bow and stern sections of the ship lie 600 m (1,970 ft) apart on the seabed, facing opposite directions. The rusty bow (right) sank deep into the mud but looms out, remarkably intact.

RESTING PLACE
The *Titanic* was found some 21 km (13 miles) away from her last recorded position in 3,800 m (12,470 ft) of water. At this depth, there is no light, no plants grow, and few fish can survive the intense pressure and cold.

SUBMERSIBLE SEARCH
In 1987, the French organization that had worked with Ballard teamed up with another US company. This time a manned submersible, the *Nautile*, went down to the wreck and, using the vessel's mechanical arms, retrieved hundreds of objects from the site.

CANADA

New York

departs Southampton 10th April

Queenstown

Cherbourg

sinks 15th April

ATLANTIC OCEAN

WHAT HAPPENED?

The discovery of the wreck in two pieces, some distance apart on the seabed and facing opposite directions, confirms that the hull broke up as she sank.

STAGE 1

As the watertight compartments filled with water one by one, the bow sank slowly, pulling the stern upwards.

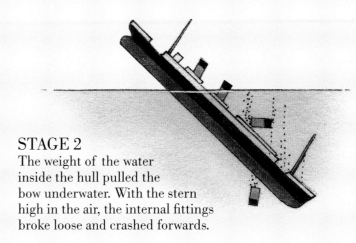

STAGE 2

The weight of the water inside the hull pulled the bow underwater. With the stern high in the air, the internal fittings broke loose and crashed forwards.

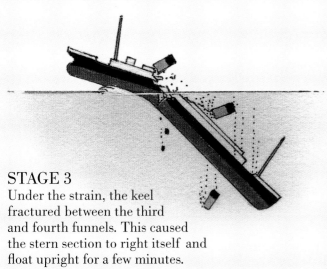

STAGE 3

Under the strain, the keel fractured between the third and fourth funnels. This caused the stern section to right itself and float upright for a few minutes.

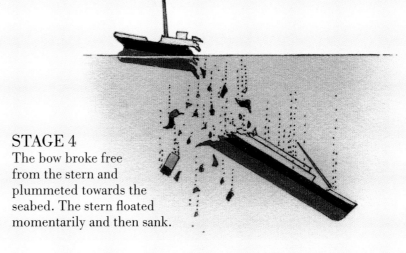

STAGE 4

The bow broke free from the stern and plummeted towards the seabed. The stern floated momentarily and then sank.

PICKING UP THE PIECES

The *Nautile* had two mechanical arms, which the pilot used for gathering objects from the seabed. In the picture above, an arm lifts a piece of one of the ship's decorative glass windows.

ARTEFACTS

Much of the ship's contents – crockery, bottles, luggage, clothes, even sinks and floor tiles – spilled out over an area known as the debris field, of nearly 2 sq km (0.7 sq miles). Many objects are remarkably intact, such as this porcelain plate bearing the logo of the White Star Line.

CONTROVERSY

The salvage of artefacts from the *Titanic* has proved controversial. Some people believe the wreck should be left in peace as a memorial, and that recovering objects, such as this purser's bag (left), is like robbing a grave. Others want to retrieve the remarkable historical objects before they disintegrate.

GLOSSARY

A la carte restaurant
A restaurant where diners can choose what they would like to eat from the menu, rather than eating a set menu.

Boat deck
The deck on which the lifeboats are stored.

Boiler
A large container for heating water with a coal fire. The steam produced powers the ship..

Bosun
An officer in command of the ship's deck crew.

Bow
The front part of a ship.

Bridge
The control centre of ship from which she is navigated.

Bulkhead
A solid wall to stop fire or flooding.

Cabin
A room on a ship where passengers sleep.

Collapsible
A lifeboat with canvas sides that collapse for easy storage.

Crow's nest
A lookout platform high up on the foremast.

Davit
One of a pair of cranes, fitted with pulleys and ropes, used to lower lifeboats.

Ensign
A flag distinguishing the country of the ship's registry.

Fireman
A person who feeds a ship's boilers with coal.

Fitting out
Installing the decks, machinery, and other equipment inside a ship's empty hull.

Forecastle
A short raised deck at the front of a ship.

Foremast
The mast nearest the front of a ship.

Funnel
A tall chimney through which smoke from the engine can escape.

Gangway
A passageway into a ship.

Gantry
A frame structure raised around something so that it can be built or serviced.

Greaser
A semi-skilled worker who attends to a ship's engine.

Hull
The main body of a ship.

Hydraulic machine
A machine that works by using the pressure of liquids, usually oil.

Life jacket
A device used to keep a person afloat in the water.

Liner
A large passenger ship that sails fixed routes, or "lines".

Log
A detailed record of a ship's voyage.

Lookout
A member of the crew who stands in the crow's nest on the foremast to keep watch for other ships or obstacles ahead.

Marconi room
A room where wireless operators worked, using a communications system devised by Italian inventor Guglielmo Marconi.

Mess
A place where a ship's crew can eat and relax.

Morse code
A telegraph code used to send messages using a system of dots and dashes to represent letters and numbers.

Morse lamp
A lamp used to transmit messages by flashing a light.

Orlop deck
The lowest deck on a ship.

Poop deck
A raised deck at the stern of a ship.

Port
The left-hand side of a ship.

Porthole
A small, usually round, window in the side of a ship.

Promenade
A deck area where passengers can walk and take the sea air.

Propeller
A device with angled blades that turn in the water to move a ship forwards.

Purser
An officer responsible for looking after money and sometimes valuables.

Quartermaster
A ship's officer whose duties include steering the ship.

Quay
A platform next to the water for loading and unloading ships.

Rivet
A short metal bolt that fastens two pieces of metal together.

Royal Mail Ship
A ship with a contract to carry British mail.

Rudder
A vertical device at the rear of a ship used for steering.

Saloon
The name for a large public room on a ship.

Shoring
A set of props used to support a structure.

Slipway
A ramp that extends out into the water so that ships can be moved in and out of the water.

Starboard
The right-hand side of a ship.

Stern
The rear end of a ship.

Steward/stewardess
A person who looks after the passengers on a ship.

Submersible
A small submarine launched from a ship.

Suite
A series of connected rooms.

Tender
A boat that carries things between a larger ship and the shore.

Trimmer
A person who breaks up large lumps of coal for a boiler.

Turkish bath
A steam bath.

Well deck
The area of the open deck of a ship between the bridge and the forecastle.

Wireless
The old-fashioned term for a radio.

INDEX

CREDITS

DK would like to thank:
Stephanie Pliakas for proofreading and Jackie Brind for the index.

The Publisher would like to thank the following for their kind permission to reproduce their photographs:

=above, c=centre, b=below, l=left, =right, t=top

8 Corbis: Bettmann (cra). 9 Mary Evans Picture Library. Rex Features: (cla). 10 Mary Evans Picture Library: Onslow Auctions Limited (cl). Rex Features: Nils Jorgensen (tr). 10-11 Getty Images: UniversalImagesGroup (cb). 11 Corbis: The Mariners' Museum (tr). National Maritime Museum, Greenwich, London: S B. Guion (tl). National Museums of Northern Ireland: Robert John Welch (br) 36 Corbis: (bc); Bettmann (cla). Dorling Kindersley: Southampton City Cultural

Services (c). Mary Evans Picture Library: (tr). 37 Corbis: Bettmann (tr). Getty Images: Archive Holdings Inc (bl). Rex Features: (br). TopFoto.co.uk: The Granger Collection (cr). 38 Alamy Images: Mary Evans Picture Library (br). Corbis: (tl). Library Of Congress, Washington, D.C.: cph 3c21013 (bl). Mary Evans Picture Library: (cra). 39 Corbis: Bettmann (bl). Getty Images: Topical Press Agency / Stringer (crb). Illustrated London News Picture Library: (tr). 40 Alamy Images: Mary

Evans Picture Library (br). Mary Evans Picture Library: Onslow Auctions Limited (tr). TopFoto. co.uk: (cb, bl, cla). 41 Corbis: (cr, tl); Bettmann (clb). 42 Corbis: (cb); Ralph White (cra). 43 Corbis: Ralph White (bl, bc). Rex Features: (crb). 45 Rex Features: (br)

All other images © Dorling Kindersley
For further information see:
www.dkimages.com